THE WAY WE ATE

100 Chefs Celebrate
a Century at the American Table

NOAH FECKS + PAUL WAGTOUICZ

A Touchstone Book

Published by Simon & Schuster

New York   London   Toronto   Sydney   New Delhi

Touchstone
A Division of Simon & Schuster, Inc.
1230 Avenue of the Americas
New York, NY 10020

First Touchstone hardcover edition November 2013

TOUCHSTONE and colophon are registered trademarks of Simon & Schuster, Inc.

For information about special discounts for bulk purchases, please contact
Simon & Schuster Special Sales at 1-866-506-1949 or business@simonandschuster.com.

The Simon & Schuster Speakers Bureau can bring authors to your live event.
For more information or to book an event contact the
Simon & Schuster Speakers Bureau at 866-248-3049
or visit our website at www.simonspeakers.com.

Designed by Teresa Hopkins
Additional illustrations by Lauren Hom

Manufactured in the United States of America

1   3   5   7   9   10   8   6   4   2

Library of Congress Cataloging-in-Publication Data

The Way We Ate / [compiled by] Noah Fecks + Paul Wagtouicz.
pages cm
"A Touchstone Book."
1. Cooking. 2. Cooking—History—20th century.
3. Popular culture—United States—History—20th century.
I. Fecks, Noah, editor of compilation. II. Wagtouicz, Paul, editor of compilation.
TX714.W2927 2013
641.50973'0904—dc23
2013015938

ISBN 978-1-4767-3272-5
ISBN 978-1-4767-3275-6 (ebook)

For Evelyn and Vito, Geraldine and Robert

✦ CONTENTS ✦

Acknowledgments

NOAH + PAUL WOULD LIKE TO THANK:

Stephanie Anderson, Heather Barbod, Evan Barbour, Amanda Barney and Matthew Orr, Melanie Belkin, Madeline Block, Lauren Bloomberg, Cheryl Brown, Jacque Burke, Robert Chistensen, Linnea Covington, Sara Demian, Hillary Dixler, Sky Dylan-Robbins, Lucinda East, Samantha Felix, Camilla Ferenczi, Norma Galehouse, Evy Gonzales, Robin Gould and Mark Jordan, Tina Heath-Schuttenberg, Lily Hodge, Lauren Hom, John Hopkins, Teresa Hopkins, Michelle Howry, Jono Jarrett, Olga Katsnelson, Kristen Kelly, Jennifer Kim, Nina Kocher, Eric Korsh and Ginevra Iverson, Dana Lapan, Emily Learnard, Amy Lombardi, Leyla Marchetto, Keith Marran, Patty McAvoy, Molly McDonald, Alexandra Norindr, the Orient Country Store, Sunny Ozell, Cassandre Pallas, Jen Pelka, Chris Ramey and Tara DiGiovanni, Charlotte Robertson, Allison and Matt Robicelli, Jennifer Rodstrom, Brian Roof, Jessica Rosen, Helen Rosner, AJ Schaller, Jill Schulster, Ruth Schultz, Tina Schuttenberg, Carla Siegel, Anna Stockwell, Kate Telfeyan, Samantha Ullrich, Seth Unger, Paul Vitale, Rachel Walensky, Katharine Woodward, and Olivia Young.

Special thanks: Allegra Ben-Amotz

FOREWORD

◆

I F YOU'VE LIVED LONG ENOUGH, AND HAVE OBSESSED OVER FOOD LONG ENOUGH, you can pinpoint the precise moments in your lifetime when certain foods "happened." Paella was very pre-rock 1960s, for example: the go-to dinner-party dish of your parents when they were acting the part of young sophisticates, playing Miles Davis's LP *Sketches of Spain* on the hi-fi while their guests, in shift dresses and skinny-lapeled suits, exulted in the mussely vapors rising from the enameled Dansk serving bowl. The mid-aughts were when charcuterie officially happened, remember? Like, how, it was 2006, and, all of a sudden, every neo-*rustico* joint offered an assortment of "house-cured *salumi*," inevitably served on a plank of wood? Balsamic vinegar most definitely happened in 1983, the summer of: that weekend you were at the beach house of your yuppie older cousin—the one who married an architect and had been repeatedly to Tuscany and Emilia-Romagna. She drizzled some syrupy-looking liquid over some toasted pieces of bread smeared with raw cheese. You said, in awe and wonderment, "What are these?" She replied, coolly and offhandedly, "Crostini with goat cheese, sautéed leek, and balsamic vinegar." You thought, *There is a whole world out there that I know nothing about.*

Er, forgive the lapse from the universal into the personal—it's just that food and drink are so inexorably caught up in memory and, therefore, in specific time periods. The curators of this book, Noah Fecks and Paul Wagtouicz, understand this. What they have cleverly *not* done, in the course of compiling recipes to represent every year of the twentieth century, is take the literalist, food-museum approach: *Here is an old recipe from 1921, here's one from 1942, and here's one from 1997.* Rather, they have gone for culinary impressionism, taking the *idea* of a specific year and then inviting a chef or an otherwise distinguished food person to translate that year—its events, its ethos, its salient gastrocultural qualities—into a beautifully realized dish or drink. (And beautifully presented, too; the curators are expert food photographers.)

In some cases, you wind up with offerings that might have indeed been served in the period in question. Both Pichet Ong's minty-green Grasshopper Ice Box Cake (1954) and Nicole Taylor's Lemon Coconut Stack Cake (1940)—the latter garnished with gardenias in homage to Hattie McDaniel, who wore gardenias in her hair when she took home the Oscar for Best Supporting Actress that year—are confections you could see being hefted out of a big ol' Norge Royal Rollator fridge and served on Fiestaware. Claudia Gonson's eponymous Claudia's Crunchy Salad (1970) is marvelously evocative of crunchier, earthier times, when patchwork denim was socially acceptable and Cat Stevens's "Morning Has Broken" was all over the radio.

Yet other participants in this book use their assigned year as a leaping-off point for more fanciful preparations. Would you have found Leah Cohen's Braised Beef Cheeks with Carrot Puree, Candy-Stripe Beets, and Tarragon on a restaurant menu in 1907? Most likely not. But 1907 was the year that the pioneering Lumière brothers brought their color photography process to the public, and Cohen's dish, so vivid in both its flavors and its colors, is a jolt of sensory wow—akin to the jolt that the Lumières' invention delivered in those sepiatone days. More out-there still is Joshua Marcus's Roasted Goose with Matzo Ball Gnocchi and Morels in Sherry Cream Sauce (1948), which putatively celebrates the establishment of the State of Israel but is neither kosher (it combines meat with dairy) nor orthodox (rendered goose schmalz?). It is, however, undoubtedly celebratory.

Then there are those chefs who are a living part of our own culinary history. Representing 1961, the epochal year of Julia Child's *Mastering the Art of French Cooking*, is Child's friend Jacques Pépin, whose Stuffed Quail with Grape Sauce is both the kind of dish that would have sent Julia into rapturous warbling and the kind of dish the young Pépin might have prepared in the kitchen of Henri Soulé's Le Pavillon when he first arrived in the United States. Cut to 1992, when one of the benefactors of the Francophilia that Child and Pépin fostered, Daniel Boulud, left Le Cirque to open his own place, Daniel. Boulud's Beef Shank Terrine (1993), peasant in its ingredient list but uptown in its preparation, embodies the defussified French food that he helped popularize in the nineties.

And, occasionally, there is a recipe so utterly transportive, such as Keedick Coulter's Pickled Shrimp and Tomato Aspic Picnic (1921), with the shrimp packed down in mason jars, that it summons breezy reveries of a time and place you've never even inhabited. Do I understand quite why Coulter's lunchtime twofer involuntarily conjures a vision of sunburned children riding the running boards of a 1921 Packard as it trundles along a North Carolina beachfront road? No. Do I enjoy the vision? Of course!

Good eating experiences are like that—immersive and fun. Messrs. Fecks and Wagtouicz are immersion experts, with a wonderful photographic blog, *The Way We Ate*, that finds them cooking their way through back issues of *Gourmet* magazine. Through their kitchen adventures, they have made a pretty awesome discovery: the secret of time travel. It all happens by means of this magical portal known as . . . the mouth.

—David Kamp

Georgette Farkas

Bradford McDonald

Darin & Greg Bresnitz

Julia Gartland

Eric Korsh & Ginevra Iv

Ben Pollinger

Leah Cohen

Zohar Zohar

Travis Post

Michael Laiskonis

AN AX TO GRIND

Carry Nation may be best remembered as the dour-faced woman who promoted a sober lifestyle by smashing bottles, bars, and taverns in an effort to further the temperance movement. Nation claimed that she had personally heard the voice of God, who instructed her to put an end to sinful saloons and to "Take something in your hands to throw at these places . . . and smash them!" Later, wielding an ax as her preferred method of inebriant destruction (in so-called hatchetations), she also crusaded against tobacco, fine dining, tailored clothing, and just about anything actually fun at the turn of the century. May all of us saturnalian rummies rejoice that she was unsuccessful in her efforts to deny us each our drams, dumpies, and doubles.

"I'LL HAVE WHAT G'S HAVING" COCKTAIL
GEORGETTE FARKAS

MAKES 1 QUART JUICE

For the rosemary-infused fresh pink grapefruit juice
One 6-inch or longer sprig rosemary
1 quart freshly squeezed pink grapefruit juice

MAKES 1 COCKTAIL

For the cocktail
3 ounces rosemary-infused fresh pink grapefruit juice
1 ounce vodka
½ ounce St-Germain elderflower liqueur
Splash fresh lemon juice
1 sprig fresh rosemary, to garnish

Prepare the rosemary-infused grapefruit juice: Place a sprig of fresh rosemary in a quart of juice and steep for 24 hours, refrigerated. Of course, you could infuse the vodka instead, but then you wouldn't have rosemary-scented grapefruit juice in your fridge, and that would be a shame.

Prepare the cocktail: Pour the ingredients into a cocktail shaker with ice and let it rip. Strain into a highball glass and garnish with a sprig of fresh rosemary as a stirrer.

NOTE: As the sweetness of fresh grapefruit juice can vary widely from batch to batch and season to season, adjust the amount of lemon juice accordingly. Personally, I prefer this cocktail nice and tart.

"This is the very first cocktail I created for the Rôtisserie," Georgette says. "While some might think it a shame to forgo the vodka, I like the virgin version just as much as

the original, with the rosemary-infused grapefruit juice simply splashed over ice and topped off with bubbly water. Carry Nation would approve."

Georgette Farkas *is the hospitality visionary behind Rôtisserie Georgette on New York City's Upper East Side, where perfectly roasted chicken is elevated to new heights. Decades of working side by side with Daniel Boulud under his Dinex umbrella honed her reputation as one of the most respected names in the business and taught her much about cocktails and divining a balanced palate of sour, sweet, bitter, and boozy in every sip.*

FLY ME TO THE MOON

Le Voyage dans la Lune, widely considered the first example of science fiction film, is an emblem of French cinema based on the novels of Jules Verne and H. G. Wells, that sparked off a worldwide fascination with fantasy, travel, and science. Predating an actual visit to Earth's majestic satellite by over half a century, the film depicts a celebratory voyage fraught with velvet waistcoats and European dancing girls, whose heroic travelers only narrowly escape death and disaster at the hands of lunar aliens. The film remains a benchmark from the silent era and set the stage for a century of Trekkies, comic book freaks, Carl Sagan fanatics, and geek culture at large.

FRICASSÉE DE VOLAILLE, ESCARGOTS, ET CHANTERELLES AU VERJUS, PAIN PERDU AUX CROISSANTS

CHICKEN, SNAILS, AND CHANTERELLE FRICASSEE WITH SAVORY CROISSANT BREAD PUDDING

BRADFORD McDONALD

Prepare the pain perdu: Preheat the oven to 325°F.

Gently bring the milk to a simmer. Remove from the heat and add the garlic, thyme, and nutmeg; infuse for 5 minutes. Strain the milk. Beat the eggs well. Stir in half the milk to temper, then the remainder. Season lightly with salt and pepper. Strain the savory anglaise.

Dice the croissants into roughly shaped ½-inch cubes. Pour the savory anglaise over them and allow to soak for 1 minute. Drain off any excess liquid, although you still want the mix to be very wet. Line the loaf pan with parchment paper along the bottom.

MAKES 6 SERVINGS

For the pain perdu
1 cup milk
1 clove garlic
1 sprig thyme
Pinch grated nutmeg
3 eggs
Salt and freshly ground black pepper
2 stale croissants
2 tablespoons clarified butter

For the snail butter
4 tablespoons butter, softened
  (en pommade, as they say)
1 tablespoon finely grated
  Parmesan cheese
1 tablespoon whole-grain Dijon mustard
2 tablespoons finely diced country ham
1 tablespoon verjus
½ teaspoon minced finely garlic

For the fricassee
3 pounds skin-on, bone-in chicken
  drumsticks and thighs
Salt and cracked black pepper
¼ cup canola oil
2 shallots, minced
1 stalk celery, minced
2 cloves garlic, minced
1 pound wild mushrooms
  (preferably chanterelles and/or morels)
Two 7-ounce cans snails, drained
  and rinsed
1 cup verjus
1 quart chicken stock
1 sprig thyme
1 fresh bay leaf
2 tablespoons minced fresh chervil
2 tablespoons minced fresh chives
Bouquet of thyme and other fresh herbs,
  for garnish

Pack in the soaked croissant and anglaise mixture. Cover with aluminum foil. Bake in a roasting pan, with water halfway up the sides of the loaf pan, for 30 to 35 minutes, until the bread takes on a spongy touch. Remove from the oven, allow to cool, then chill. Unmold and slice into 6 even portions. Reserve for later.

Prepare the snail butter: Mix all ingredients together in a small bowl until well combined. Chill and reserve for later.

Prepare the fricassee: Very lightly season the chicken with a small pinch of salt and cracked black pepper. In a large Dutch oven, brown the chicken skin side down in the canola oil over medium-high heat. Once browned, remove from the pan.

Degrease the pan of the excess oil without removing the *fond* (caramelization at the bottom of the pan). Add the shallots, celery, and garlic over medium heat. The moisture in the vegetables should begin to deglaze the fond. Using a wooden spatula, scrape the fond away and sweat the vegetables without letting them color.

Add the mushrooms and sauté lightly. If they release moisture, cook until the pan is almost dry again. Add the snails. Deglaze with the verjus and allow to come to a simmer. Add the chicken stock and allow to return to a simmer. Add the chicken back into the pot along with the thyme and bay leaf. Cover and let simmer gently for 30 to 35 minutes.

Uncover and remove and reserve the chicken, snails, and mushrooms. Discard the thyme and bay leaf. Boil the liquid to reduce rapidly to half. Add the snail butter to the reduced liquid and bring to a simmer to create an emulsion that has viscosity but is not soupy. Adjust the seasoning with salt and cracked black pepper.

Return the reserved ingredients to the pot and coat generously in the sauce.

Just before serving, add the chervil and chives.

To serve: Fry the pain perdu slices lightly in the clarified butter in a nonstick pan until caramelized.

Arrange the dish on a platter for table space. Garnish with the herb bouquet.

Special equipment

7½ by 3½ by 2¼-inch nonstick loaf pan
Parchment paper
Roasting pan
4-quart Dutch oven

Brad's entrée is a sublime combination of fantasy, fiction, and all things French. "I thought immediately of croissants," he says. "The crescent moon–shaped objects, as Brillat-Savarin would have agreed, are perfect for a savory bread pudding." Replacing the traditional white wine with verjus gives this dish a higher acid content that helps cut through the fat to produce more tender chicken and ensure maximum deliciousness.

Husband and father **Brad McDonald** *is a southern chef who cut his teeth at some of the leading restaurants in the world and made his mark as executive chef at the famed (albeit short-lived) Governor Restaurant in Brooklyn, New York.*

WHEN PIG FLIES

Ohio brothers Wilbur and Orville Wright's successful bicycle business didn't really take off until 1903, when their growing interest in aeronautical experimentation led to their first powered flight at Kill Devil Hills, North Carolina. In the years spent preparing for their great adventure, days of inclement weather would often send the pair back indoors to tinker with their machines. Here is a down-home, hearty feast that would have sustained two mechanically minded minds through days that weren't quite right for flight, save for this bit of porcine delight taking off from their plates.

RAINY SUNDAY PORK SHOULDER WITH SESAME COLE SLAW
DARIN & GREG BRESNITZ

Prepare the pork shoulder: Combine the water, sugar, salt, peppercorns, chili flakes, and mustard in a large container. Submerge the pork shoulder, cover, and refrigerate at least 12 hours or up to 48 hours.

Preheat oven to 300°F.

Melt the butter in a heavy-bottomed roasting pan over medium heat. Add the apples and sauté until soft. Push them toward the sides of the pan. Remove the pork from the brine, brush away any excess, and pat it dry with paper towels. Place the pork in the center of the pan and sear it well on all sides, ending with the fat side facing up. Use a knife to slice a crosshatch diamond pattern ¼ to ½ inch into the fat, taking care not to expose the meat below it. Fill the pan with cider until it reaches 1 to 1½ inches up the sides of the pork. Cover the pan with foil. Roast for 7 to 8 hours, basting the pork once every hour with the braising liquid. Once the pork is tender enough to easily shred with a fork, coat the pork with dark brown sugar. Set the oven to broil and cook, uncovered, until the sugar has caramelized.

MAKES 8 TO 10 SERVINGS

For the pork shoulder

6 cups warm water

2 cups dark brown sugar, plus more as needed

2 cups kosher salt

½ cup whole black peppercorns

½ cup chili flakes or powder

½ cup dry mustard

One 8- to 10-pound bone-in pork shoulder, rind removed

¼ pound unsalted butter

3 pounds McIntosh apples, peeled, cored, and quartered

1 to 2 quarts sparkling apple cider

Potato rolls or other bread, for serving

For the sesame cole slaw

1 large shallot, thinly sliced

2 tablespoons kosher salt

Juice of 1 large lime

½ cup sesame seeds

2 cups shredded carrots

2 cups shredded red cabbage

2 cups shredded green cabbage

About 1 cup mayonnaise (Kewpie preferred)

1 tablespoon freshly ground black pepper

1 teaspoon sweet paprika

1 teaspoon ground Himalayan pink salt

Remove the pork from the roasting pan and set aside. If there is substantial braising liquid left in the pan, blend it with a hand-held blender until smooth and reduce over medium heat to one-half to one-fourth its original volume to make a dipping sauce.

Prepare the sesame cole slaw: While the pork is cooking, combine the shallot with the kosher salt and set aside for 30 minutes to draw out bitterness. Rinse off the salt completely, drain, then mix the shallot with the lime juice and let stand 30 minutes. Lightly toast the sesame seeds in a dry pan and set aside to cool. Combine the carrots, red and green cabbage, and shallot in a large bowl and mix with mayonnaise—more for a creamier consistency, less for a drier slaw. Add the pepper, paprika, Himalayan salt, and sesame seeds while continuing to toss. Mix until fully incorporated. Refrigerate until ready to serve.

Shred the pork shoulder with the tines of a fork on a large serving platter, board, or dish. Discard the bone, or fight over who gets to suck it. Serve the pork with the cole slaw, dipping sauce, and potato rolls or your bread of choice. ✥

Twin brothers **Darin and Greg Bresnitz** *have traveled the world as the consulting team Finger on the Pulse, bringing New York's music and food cultures to points beyond. They are the creators of the IFC television show* Dinner with the Band *and weekly radio show* Snacky Tunes, *where they explore the intersection between food and music, as well as their popular Summer BBQ Blowout Series, where Brooklyn's culture vultures stuff their faces in the heat of the summer night, set to live music. When they're not hustling to bring the party to the people, Finger on the Pulse has been known to enjoy good whiskey, cheap whiskey, and all the whiskeys in between.*

A BOWL OF CHERRIES

MAKES 6 TO 8 SERVINGS

For the topping

1 cup chopped walnuts

⅔ cup gluten-free rolled oats

⅓ cup brown sugar,
  plus more for dusting

¼ cup almond meal

¼ cup corn flour (fine masa harina)

¼ cup sorghum flour

¼ cup gluten-free all-purpose flour
  (such as Bob's Red Mill)

¼ teaspoon fine sea salt

⅛ teaspoon freshly grated nutmeg

8 tablespoons plus 1 teaspoon unsalted
  butter, chilled and cubed

For the filling

3 cups pitted cherries, fresh or
  frozen and drained

½ cup granulated sugar

2 tablespoons tapioca starch

1 teaspoon vanilla extract

⅛ teaspoon freshly grated nutmeg

Unsalted butter, for the pan

The Cherry Orchard was the handsome and iconic playwright Anton Chekhov's final work for the stage. Intended as a comedy, the play combines elements of humor and tragedy into a grand irony that can only be called "Chekhovian," as the characters oscillate between slapstick humor and pained sadness. The play, which premiered on the Moscow stage in January 1904, proved an unintended coda to Chekhov's career, as he succumbed to tuberculosis just a few months later at the age of forty-four. *The Cherry Orchard* has since undergone several incarnations under countless directors in a multitude of languages. Its unique, visionary approach to presenting the highs and lows of human experience has kept the piece in production almost continuously for over a century.

WHOLE-GRAIN SWEET CHERRY CRUMBLE
(GLUTEN FREE)
JULIA GARTLAND

Prepare the topping: Stir together the walnuts, oats, brown sugar, almond meal, and corn, sorghum, and all-purpose flours in a large bowl. Whisk in the salt and nutmeg. Add 8 tablespoons of the butter and combine well, using your hands to work in the cubes. The topping will become crumbly and moist. Set aside.

Prepare the filling: Combine the cherries in a medium bowl with the sugar, tapioca starch, and vanilla. Mix gently until the dry ingredients absorb the liquid. Stir in the nutmeg. Lightly coat a baking dish with butter. Pour in the filling.

Assemble and bake the crumble: Preheat the oven to 350°F. Crumble the topping over the filling. Top with the remaining

1 teaspoon butter and dust with brown sugar. Bake for 45 minutes to 1 hour, until the fruit is bubbling and the crumble topping is golden. Cool for 20 minutes before serving. 🪶

Julia Gartland *is the cook and photographer behind the blog* Sassy Kitchen. *She cooks, shoots, and eats (gluten-free) out of Brooklyn, New York. Hers is an excellent alternative dessert that will please all of your guests, not just the gluten-free folks. If you can't find corn flour, Julia suggests putting cornmeal in a food processor to grind into a flour, then running this mixture through a sieve to form a fine powder.*

MIRACLE YEAR

When Albert Einstein published the *annus mirabilis* (Latin for "miracle year") papers, he shook the world's perceptions of space, matter, and time. Included in the four articles that changed the foundation of physics were his groundbreaking findings on Brownian motion, mass-energy equivalence, and his special theory of relativity, but it was his work on photoelectric effect that would eventually earn him a Nobel Prize in 1921. Diners of the time might especially relate to this electric dish, which is miraculously energizing and browned to perfection. In a word: genius.

ROASTED FOWL WITH SHALLOTS, CHANTERELLE MUSHROOMS, GARLIC CONFIT, AND VINEGAR SAUCE

ERIC KORSH & GINEVRA IVERSON

Prepare the garnish: Roast the whole shallots in a 275°F oven until completely soft and golden. Reserve.

Sauté the chanterelles in the olive oil over medium-high heat with a pinch of salt and pepper. When the chanterelles are light gold, add the diced shallot, the garlic, and butter. Cook until the chanterelles are deep gold. Cool on paper towels.

Prepare the garlic confit: Put the garlic cloves in plenty of cold water and bring to a boil. Let the cloves boil hard for 1 minute. Do this three times, discarding the water each time. Finally, cover the soft, sweet cloves in a small amount of extra virgin olive oil. Reserve.

Prepare the sauce: Chop the quail heads, necks, and feet into small pieces. (Reserve the quail bodies.) If there aren't enough bones to cover the bottom of a small rondeau, supplement with

MAKES 4 SERVINGS

For the garnish
12 whole medium shallots, peeled
16 medium chanterelles
  (select mushrooms that are firm, dry, and aromatic)
2 tablespoons olive oil
Salt and freshly ground black pepper
1 shallot, cut in ⅛-inch dice
4 cloves garlic, minced
2 tablespoons unsalted butter

For the garlic confit
12 cloves garlic, peeled
Extra virgin olive oil

For the sauce
Heads, necks, and feet from 8 quail
Chopped chicken bones (optional)
2 tablespoons duck fat
4 shallots, diced small
4 stalks celery, diced small
2 medium carrots, diced small
1 head garlic, cloves separated and chopped
2 cups white wine
1 quart rich chicken stock
1 sprig thyme
2 tablespoons unsalted butter, chilled and cubed
Good-quality sherry vinegar
Salt and freshly ground black pepper

For the fowl
Salt and freshly ground black pepper
8 quail, plucked and gutted
Fresh thyme leaves
Duck fat
Unsalted butter

chicken bones. On the stove, in just enough duck fat to cover the bottom of the rondeau, brown all the bones evenly. Remove the bones, drain in a colander, and reserve. Add the shallots, celery, carrots, and chopped garlic and cook until soft and with light color, taking care not to burn the bottom of the rondeau. Deglaze with the white wine, bring to a boil, and add the bones and chicken stock. Simmer for 1 hour. Pass the sauce through a sieve and while it is still hot, add the sprig of thyme to steep.

Finish the sauce right before you cook the quail. Discard the thyme sprig. Bring the sauce to a boil in a medium saucepot. Immediately remove from the heat and let the sauce relax. (**NOTE:** Butter emulsifies well into a sauce close to 180°F.) Swirl the butter into the sauce while adding a few teaspoons of good sherry vinegar (to taste). The sauce should be sharp but not overpowering. Season to taste with salt and pepper. Reserve, keeping warm.

Prepare the fowl: Salt and pepper the quail and stuff the cavities with a small pinch of thyme leaves. In a heavy pan, roast the birds in duck fat and butter until they are golden on the outside but pink in the middle. Do not overcook.

To serve: Place the chanterelles, garlic confit, roasted shallots, and sauce on a large plate or shallow bowl. Arrange the quail on top.

NOTE: Ideally, a red-legged partridge would be used for this: shot and hung for a week, roasted rare, and finished, after breaking the bird into quarters, in duck fat. Quail, however, make a fine substitute as red-legged partridge are available only September through December.

Eric Korsh *and* **Ginevra Iverson** *are the husband-wife owner-chef team at Calliope in New York City's East Village, where they are leading a renewed obsession with French cuisine, turning out an authentic vintage-before-vintage menu and impeccable standard of service. Eric notched his knife at the iconic Waverly Inn in the West Village, Patio Dining, Jerry's, Patroon, and Café des Artistes; Ginevra has consulted for restaurants and been a private chef, with tenures at Prune and Jack's Luxury Oyster Bar. The two met while working at Picholine on the Upper West Side, and went on to found their first restaurant together, a French-Mediterranean destination spot called Restaurant Eloise in Sonoma County, California.*

GRAND HOTEL

MAKES 4 SERVINGS

For the cured salmon

One 1-pound boneless, skinless king
  salmon fillet, cut from the top of the
  fillet, with no bloodline

¼ cup raspberry vodka

10 turns of a pepper mill filled with
  black pepper, set to a very coarse grind

2 cups kosher salt

1 cup sugar

One 1-inch piece ginger, peeled
  and grated

Grated zest of 1 Meyer lemon

For the tartare

1 Meyer lemon

6 ounces king salmon belly, diced ¼ inch

¼ teaspoon coarse sel gris de Guérande

1 teaspoon Indian coriander seed, lightly
  toasted and cracked medium-fine

1 tablespoon extra virgin olive oil

Fine sea salt and freshly ground
  black pepper

For the raspberry sauce

1 cup fresh raspberries

1½-inch piece ginger, peeled

Juice of ½ Meyer lemon

¼ teaspoon fine sea salt

For the garnish

Reserved Meyer lemon zest from
  the tartare

1 tablespoon extra virgin olive oil

Watercress leaves

At the turn of the century and after the Gold Rush, San Francisco rose as a cosmopolitan center of art, society, commerce, and glamour. Its famed Palace Hotel (the largest in the West) was a true jewel of the city, known throughout the world. The original hotel, with over seven hundred opulent guest rooms, a grand atrium, and palatial dining rooms, was tragically destroyed in the famous earthquake and subsequent fires of 1906. The hotel's legacy of regal and decadent service is still credited for introducing European grandeur and elegance to America's dining culture.

RASPBERRY-CURED SALMON WITH SALMON TARTARE, GINGER, AND MEYER LEMON

BEN POLLINGER

Prepare the cured salmon: Place the salmon fillet on a plate. Pour the raspberry vodka over the salmon, then wait 5 minutes, turning once or twice. Season with black pepper.

Mix salt, sugar, ginger, and lemon zest. Place a 1 gallon zippered plastic bag flat on a tray. Lay half the salt mixture in the bag. Lay the salmon fillet on top of the salt mixture. Cover the salmon fillet with the remaining salt mixture. Seal the bag, pressing out air. Marinate in the refrigerator for 30 hours, turning every 6 hours.

Remove the salmon from the salt mixture and rinse quickly under cold water. Pat dry with paper towels. Lay on a wire rack set on a tray and place in the refrigerator overnight, uncovered. Cut the fillet approximately in half so the two pieces are at least 5 inches long each from head to tail end. Slice the salmon on approximately a 45-degree bias from the center of the fillet to the head end of the fillet. Reserve.

Prepare the tartare: Remove the yellow zest from the Meyer lemon with a vegetable peeler. Reserve. Cut the lemon in half. Squeeze and strain the juice. Combine the salmon belly with the sel gris, coriander, olive oil, lemon juice, fine sea salt, and pepper to taste.

Lay out 4 sheets of plastic wrap, 8 inches long, on a table. Arrange 3 slices of cured salmon on each sheet, overlapping by 1 inch. Divide the tartare among the 4 sheets on the edge closest to you, about ½ inch from the edge of the cured salmon. Roll, using the plastic wrap, as if rolling sushi. (Be sure once one full rotation of the roll has been made that you gradually pull back the plastic wrap so you don't roll it into the salmon roll.) Slice the ends of each roll on a 45-degree angle. Wrap tightly in plastic. Reserve.

Prepare the raspberry sauce: Combine all the ingredients and blend smooth in a blender. Strain. Reserve.

Prepare the garnish: Cut the Meyer lemon zest, with no pith, in fine brunoise (1/16-inch square). Combine the zest with the oil.

To plate: Pour the raspberry sauce onto a plate as desired. Unwrap the salmon rolls and arrange atop the sauce. Coat the salmon rolls lightly with the lemon zest oil. Sprinkle with watercress. 🌿

Ben's discovery of an 1876 menu from the Palace Hotel, which included Salmon à la Chambord, inspired his dish. "The name Chambord," he says, "has become synonymous with raspberries and was inspired by a liqueur served at the Château de Chambord in the Loire Valley. I've paid homage to the concept of the ingredients and given it my take by curing a fillet of salmon in the style of gravlax, with the addition of raspberry vodka." The combination of fruit and salmon makes for a grand, memorable meal that's worth every effort.

New Jersey native **Ben Pollinger** *began his culinary career under Chef Alain Ducasse at the Monte Carlo institution Le Louis XV. He is currently the executive chef of the inventive, delicious, and celebrated Oceana.*

SATURATION POINT

Auguste and Louis Lumière perfected the first color photography process to reach a mass market audience. Known as Autochrome, the process used a glass plate coated with a mosaic of microscopic grains of potato starch dyed red-orange, green, and blue-violet, with a black carbon material filling the spaces between them, to act as color filters before the light transmitted through a lens reached the emulsion. There was considerable light loss in this process and the finished slide was rather dark but still vividly colorful. Leah Cohen's pan-Asian fare is a feast for the eyes, activating a similar vibrant palette in one's mouth.

BRAISED BEEF CHEEKS WITH CARROT PUREE, CANDY-STRIPE BEETS, AND TARRAGON
LEAH COHEN

Prepare the braised beef cheeks: Preheat the oven to 325°F. Heat the oil in a heavy, ovenproof pot over moderately high heat until hot but not smoking. While the oil is heating, pat the beef cheeks dry and season generously with salt and pepper. Brown the beef on all sides and remove from the pot. Pour off excess fat from the pot, leaving only 3 tablespoons. Add the onion, carrot, and celery and sauté over medium heat. Once the vegetables are tender, add the garlic and cook for 2 minutes more. Stir in the tomato paste and cook for 3 minutes, stirring constantly to prevent burning. Deglaze with the wine, making sure to scrape up all of the bits stuck on the bottom of the pan. Reduce the liquid by half. Add the beef stock. Return the cheeks, with any juices, to the pot. Bring to a simmer, then braise, covered, in the middle of the oven until very tender, approximately 3 hours. Let the cheeks cool down in the braising liquid. Once cool, remove the beef and strain the liquid. (This liquid will become the sauce.) In a saucepan, reduce the liquid until it is thick

MAKES 4 TO 6 SERVINGS

For the braised beef cheeks
¼ cup extra virgin olive oil
12 ounces clean beef cheeks
Salt and freshly ground black pepper
1 medium onion, finely chopped
1 medium carrot, finely chopped
2 stalks celery, finely chopped
5 cloves garlic, peeled and smashed
2 tablespoons tomato paste
2 cups dry red wine
3 cups beef stock
2 tablespoons unsalted butter, cold

For the carrot puree
1 tablespoon canola oil
1 shallot, thinly sliced
2 small cloves garlic, smashed
½ pound carrots, cut into medium pieces
⅓ cup chicken stock
Salt
2 tablespoons heavy cream
1 tablespoon brown butter

For the beets
½ teaspoon Dijon mustard
2 tablespoons extra virgin olive oil
1 tablespoon freshly squeezed
  lemon juice
Pinch sugar
Salt and freshly ground black pepper
2 small candy-stripe beets, cleaned,
  peeled, and sliced very thin (or a
  colorful assortment of seasonal beets)
2 tablespoons fresh tarragon leaves

enough to coat the back of a spoon. Whisk in the butter and adjust seasoning to taste. Keep warm.

Prepare the carrot puree: Heat the canola oil in a saucepan. Add the shallot and garlic and sweat for 3 minutes. Add the carrots and chicken stock; season with salt; and cook, covered, until the carrots are very tender, 12 to 14 minutes. Puree the carrots with the heavy cream and brown butter in a blender. Adjust the seasoning.

Prepare the beets: In a medium bowl, combine the mustard, olive oil, lemon juice, sugar, and salt and pepper to taste. Toss the candy-stripe beets in this vinaigrette and coat well. Sprinkle with tarragon leaves to garnish.

To serve: Arrange thin slices of beef cheek on a plate in a fan, topped with sauce. Add carrot puree and beets for bursts of color, and garnish with fresh tarragon or a similar herb. 🌾

Leah Cohen *brings the vibrant flavors of Southeast Asian street food to New York's Lower East Side with her pioneering and authentic menu at Pig and Khao. An alum of Eleven Madison Park, David Burke's Park Avenue Café, La Madia in Sicily, and Anne Burrell's Centro Vinoteca, Leah also made a successful run on television's* Top Chef *before embarking on a yearlong tour spanning Hong Kong, Thailand, Vietnam, the Philippines, and Malaysia to glean inspiration for her latest venture.*

TO MOTHER YOU

MAKES 2 SMALL LOAVES

Unsalted butter, for the pans

7 ounces (¾ cup plus 2 tablespoons)
  pitted dates (see Note)

3½ ounces (⅓ cup plus 3 tablespoons)
  raw shelled almonds

3½ ounces (⅓ cup plus 3 tablespoons)
  raw shelled pecans

½ cup sugar

¾ cup all-purpose flour

2 large eggs

West Virginian Anna Jarvis orchestrated the nation's first Mother's Day holiday in remembrance of her own mother, Anna Reeves Jarvis, who had been an advocate for mothers of soldiers on both sides of the Civil War to unite against the atrocities of battle, treat their sons' wounds with neutrality, and organize for peace. But once President Woodrow Wilson declared Mother's Day an official national holiday some years later in 1914, daughter Anna became disillusioned with the popular charge to commercialize it. "I wanted it to be a day of sentiment, not profit," she said, and opposed the sale of flowers, calling the use of printed greeting cards "a poor excuse for the letter you are too lazy to write." The following recipe is dedicated to Anna's resolve to elevate those women who matter most in all of our lives.

LOVE LOAF
ZOHAR ZOHAR

Preheat the oven to 350°F. Butter 2 small loaf pans and line them with parchment paper. In a large bowl, mix the fruit and nuts. In another bowl, mix the sugar, flour, and eggs into a smooth batter. Pour the batter over the fruit and nut mixture and combine well. Pour into the prepared pans. Bake 40 to 50 minutes, rotating the pans after 25 minutes.

Remove the loaves from the oven when they are dark golden brown and almost firm. Let sit in the pans for 10 to 15 minutes, then turn them out of the pans onto a wire rack and allow to cool completely. It is best to leave them until the next day before slicing thin with a serrated knife. Enjoy immediately or keep in an airtight container for up to 3 weeks.

NOTE: Use any other combination of dried fruit and nuts that you like, in the same weight ratio.

Zohar Zohar *brightens New York's East Village with a taste of home at Zucker Bakery. Born and raised on a kibbutz in Israel where*

residents grew most of their own food, Zohar took quickly to the joy of baking and cooking the food that nourished her community, making her first cake at age six. She fondly recalls the culture of sharing recipes and techniques among her mother, grandmother, and the other women in the kibbutz, each one known for her specialty. In the tradition of her mother and grandmother before her, the sense of family Zohar brings to her sweet and savory creations is baked right into every crisp, flaky, buttery morsel. Her love loaf is a sort of homemade energy bar that you can feel good about eating every day.

A WORLD WITHOUT LIMITS

The year 1909 brought the first photos of the remote North Pole. The Earth was still a boundless, uncharted place, and the urge to explore a revered pastime. Even Dorothy, the little girl from Kansas, was a seasoned traveler, making that year her fourth voyage to Oz. Meanwhile, in San Jose, California, a farmer's son Charles Herrold appropriated a term for casting seed in all directions when he becomes the first American to "broadcast" a radio signal to the local public. The year was filled with tributes to the American exploratory spirit, that yearning and reaching beyond what is known and seeking faraway influences in a world without limits.

BAKED ALASKA
TRAVIS POST

Prepare the pound cake base: Preheat the oven to 375°F. Butter two 9-inch round cake pans and line the bottoms with parchment paper. Sift together the salt, flour, cornstarch, and baking powder. Cream the butter and sugar together with an electric mixer on medium speed until light and fluffy, 3 to 5 minutes. Gradually add the eggs and continue to mix until well incorporated. Reduce the mixer speed to low and add the dry ingredients in 2 or 3 stages. Fold in the melted chocolate. Pour the batter into the prepared pans. Bake until firm in the center and a toothpick inserted comes out clean, 25 to 35 minutes. Allow to cool a few minutes in the pans, then turn out to cool on a wire rack. With a long bread knife, trim the cakes to an even thickness, parallel to the countertop. Reserve, or, if preparing ahead of time, wrap in plastic wrap and keep at room temperature until needed. (You will need only one of the cakes.)

Prepare the bombe: Allow the pistachio ice cream to soften on the counter approximately 30 minutes. Lightly oil the 8-inch bowl and line it with plastic wrap. Using a rubber spatula, spread the pistachio ice cream to fill the bowl, making sure to create even

MAKES 8 TO 10 SERVINGS

For the pound cake base
9 tablespoons plus 1 teaspoon unsalted butter, softened, plus more for the pans

⅜ teaspoon fine sea salt

6 ounces (1¼ cups) cake flour

1¼ ounces (¼ cup plus 1½ teaspoons) cornstarch

1⅝ teaspoons baking powder

6 ounces (¼ cup plus 1½ teaspoons) sugar

8 ounces eggs (5 large eggs)

9 ounces bittersweet chocolate, melted and cooled to room temperature

For the ice cream bombe
3 pints pistachio ice cream

Neutral oil

1 pint black cherry ice cream

For the ganache
1⅓ cups heavy cream

21 ounces bittersweet chocolate, chips or chopped

For the meringue
8 ounces (1 cup + 2 tablespoons) sugar

¼ cup water

4¼ ounces (⅓ cup) corn syrup

4¼ ounces egg whites (5 egg whites), at room temperature

Pinch salt

Special equipment
8-inch-diameter stainless-steel or glass bowl

4-inch-diameter stainless-steel or glass bowl

coverage on the sides, while leaving a small well in the center. Drape the 4-inch bowl with plastic wrap and gently push it into the center of the ice cream where you've made a well, until the top rim of the 4-inch bowl is nearly flush with the top rim of the larger bowl. Scrape off and reserve any excess pistachio ice cream. ("Ice cream sandwich with the extra chocolate cake, anyone?") Place in the freezer until the ice cream is firm, 30 to 45 minutes.

While the pistachio is firming up, let the black cherry ice cream soften.

Remove the 4-inch bowl and pull the plastic film off the pistachio ice cream. Gently spread the black cherry ice cream to fill the well created by the small bowl, leveling off the top to be level with the pistachio ice cream around it. Return to the freezer until very firm, 30 to 45 minutes.

Prepare the ganache: Bring the heavy cream to a light simmer. Pour the cream over the bittersweet chocolate in a small heatproof bowl. Allow to sit for 1 to 2 minutes, then stir until smooth. Let cool to room temperature.

With a cake spatula or long knife, scrape off any excess ice cream, to create a smooth, even surface. Pour the ganache onto the flat surface of the ice cream. Spread even. Return to the freezer to set. At this stage, cover with plastic and freeze for 2 hours or up to 3 days. Reserve additional ganache for another purpose, or as accompaniment for the extra cake as a snack throughout this lengthy preparation.

Prepare the meringue: Combine the sugar, water, and corn syrup in a small saucepan. Heat on medium, stirring until the sugar is dissolved. Without stirring, continue to heat until it reaches 240°F. When the syrup reaches approximately 220°F, begin to whip the egg whites and salt with an electric mixer on medium speed, until medium peaks are reached. When the syrup reaches 240°F, remove it from the heat and slowly add it to the egg whites, constantly mixing on medium speed. When all the syrup has been added, increase to high speed and continue to whip until stiff and glossy peaks form, 5 to 10 minutes.

Assemble: Place the ice cream bowl on the counter. Carefully place 1 layer of cake over the top. Trim the cake to fit the shape

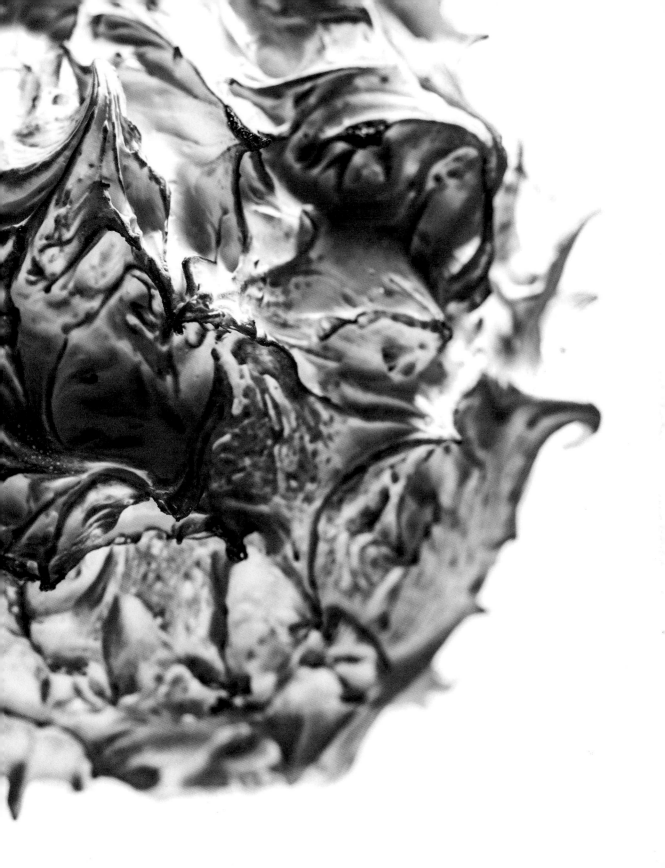

of the top of the bowl by cutting straight down along the outside of the bowl, being careful not to cut the plastic wrap lining the bowl. Place the intended serving tray or plate upside down over the cake. Grasping the top and bottom securely, invert so that the bowl is now upside down. Holding the plastic wrap, gently lift the bowl off the ice cream. (If the outer surface of the ice cream has softened, return to the freezer for 30 minutes.)

Using a spatula, evenly spread the meringue to cover the dome of ice cream, finishing with either a smooth swirl or light taps to create a stucco-like surface. Lightly toast the meringue with a handheld kitchen torch.

Serve immediately, or return to the freezer for up to 2 hours, until ready to serve. 🎋

NOTE: The pound cake and the bombe can be made up to 3 days ahead.

Travis Post *skipped cartoons as a kid, favoring programs with Martin Yan and Jacques Pépin. He jumped right into the Arizona restaurant business while still in high school, following up with training at the Culinary Institute of America and some time cooking and backpacking in Alaska. Since landing in New York, he's stopped at Cru in the West Village and Franny's in Park Slope, Brooklyn, and helped bring Bklyn Larder to life before opening minds and mouths to a seldom-represented regional Chinese cuisine at Yunnan Kitchen to great acclaim.*

FIRE AND ICE

The unusually close visit to Earth by Halley's comet in 1910 (Earth actually passed through the tail) set into motion curiosity, wonder, and a massive interest in astronomy. Sales of telescopes shot up as newspapers bore headlines that fell somewhere between "upcoming astronomical phenomenon" and "assured end of the world." The celestial visit also triggered waves of panic, hysteria, and a myriad of products designed to protect humanity from the ravages of the killer comet. So-called Comet Pills and gas masks sold hand over fist to a public that seemed convinced the tail of the comet contained toxic gas that would surely destroy all humanity. Thankfully, the people of Earth survived and will likely be awaiting the comet's return, sometime around July 2061.

THE COMET COUPE
MICHAEL LAISKONIS

Prepare the pistachio ice cream: Place the whole milk in a saucepan. Whisk in the dry milk to rehydrate it. Gently bring to a boil. Meanwhile, whisk together the sugar and egg yolks. Temper the hot milk into the yolk mixture. Return to low heat and cook, stirring, until slightly thickened, 184°F. Remove from the heat and whisk in the heavy cream and pistachio paste. Chill in an ice water bath. Allow the base to mature in the refrigerator for at least 12 hours. Process in an ice cream machine according to the manufacturer's instructions. Transfer to a covered container and allow to harden in the freezer.

Prepare the vanilla ice cream: Place the whole milk and vanilla bean and seeds in a saucepan. Whisk in the dry milk to rehydrate it. Gently bring to a boil. Meanwhile, whisk together the sugar and egg yolks. Temper the hot milk into the yolk mixture. Return to low heat and cook, stirring, until slightly thickened, 184°F. Remove from the heat and whisk in the heavy cream. Strain out and discard the vanilla bean. Chill in an ice water bath. Allow the base to mature in the refrigerator for at least 12 hours.

MAKES 8 SERVINGS

For the pistachio ice cream
2½ cups whole milk
1 tablespoon nonfat dry milk
10 tablespoons sugar
4 large egg yolks
10 tablespoons heavy cream
5 tablespoons sweetened pistachio paste

For the vanilla ice cream
2 cups whole milk
1 vanilla bean, split and scraped
1 tablespoon nonfat dry milk
10 tablespoons sugar
4 large egg yolks
6 tablespoons heavy cream

For the meringue buttons
2 large egg whites
½ cup sugar

For the caramel sauce
1 cup sugar
¼ cup water
A few drops freshly squeezed lemon juice
½ cup heavy cream
2 tablespoons unsalted butter

For the crushed raspberries
1 cup fresh raspberries
1 tablespoon sugar

For the lemon cream
2 large eggs
¾ cup sugar
½ cup freshly squeezed lemon juice
Grated zest of 1 lemon
6 tablespoons unsalted butter, diced

For assembly

1 cup fresh raspberries

½ cup pistachios, crushed

Special equipment

Instant-read thermometer

Ice cream machine

Pastry bag with medium plain tip

Process in an ice cream machine according to the manufacturer's instructions. Transfer to a covered container and allow to harden in the freezer.

Prepare the meringue buttons: Place the egg whites and sugar in a small heatproof bowl over simmering water. Stir continuously until the mixture reaches 140°F, or until the sugar has completely dissolved. Transfer to the bowl of a stand mixer and begin to whip on medium-high speed. Continue to whip until the mixer bowl is cool to the touch.

Preheat the oven to 200°F. Line a large baking sheet with parchment paper or a silicone baking mat.

Transfer the meringue to a pastry bag fitted with a medium plain tip and pipe small buttons onto the baking sheet. Place in the oven and slowly dry until crisp. Let cool on the baking sheet. Store in an airtight container.

Prepare the caramel sauce: Combine the sugar, water, and lemon juice in a small covered saucepan. Cook to a medium amber color.

Meanwhile, gently heat the cream until warm. Remove the caramelized sugar from the heat and add the cream. Return to low heat to completely dissolve the sugar. Remove from heat and allow to cool briefly. Whisk the butter into the caramel. Cover and refrigerate until needed.

Prepare the crushed raspberries: Combine the raspberries and sugar in a saucepan. Gently heat while stirring and lightly crushing the berries. Continue to cook until the sugar has dissolved into the juice released by the berries; remove from the heat and allow to cool. Chill until needed.

Prepare the lemon cream: In a heavy saucepan, whisk together the eggs and sugar. Whisk in the juice and zest. Bring to a boil over medium heat, stirring constantly, as it can easily scorch on the bottom. When the mixture just comes to a boil and is quite thick, remove from heat and whisk in the butter in small amounts. Strain through a fine-mesh sieve and chill.

Assemble the dessert: In each serving dish, place 1 spoonful each of the lemon cream and crushed raspberries, then place 2 small scoops each of the pistachio and vanilla ice cream. Top with the

"I was inspired by the simple fact that a comet is essentially ice and dust, so a frozen dessert seemed perfect—and this sundae contains a composite of some of my favorite flavors and textures."

caramel sauce, a bit more of the lemon cream and crushed raspberries, and finish with crushed pistachios, fresh raspberries, and meringue buttons.

NOTE: Ice cream can be kept frozen up to 4 days in advance; the caramel sauce, lemon cream, and crushed raspberries may be prepared and stored tightly wrapped in the refrigerator up to 4 days.

Michael Laiskonis *is the creative director of New York City's Institute of Culinary Education. He received a James Beard Award in 2007 for his work as executive pastry chef at Manhattan's Le Bernardin. "I can only imagine the sense of public awe and wonder that surrounded the passing of Halley's Comet back in 1910," he says. "These days, such astronomical events come and go with little fanfare."*

Massimiliano Nanni

Jeremiah Tower

Daniel Mattern & Roxar

Del Pedro

Allison Kave & Keavy B

Danielle Chang

Kelly Hogan

Barbara Sibley

Corey Cova

Tiffany Short